D1241545

DISCARD

21st
Century
Skills Library

REAL WORLD MATH: HEALTH AND WELLNESS

# BREAKFAST BY THE NUMBERS

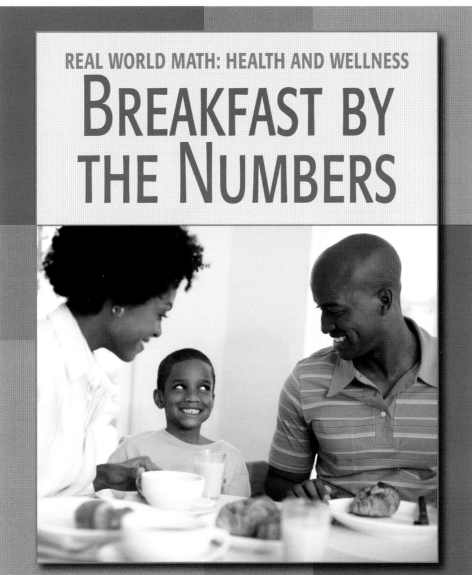

*Cecilia Minden*

PUBLIC LIBRARY
EAST ORANGE PUBLIC LIBRARY

Cherry Lake Publishing
Ann Arbor, Michigan

CHERRY LAKE
Publishing

Published in the United States of America by Cherry Lake Publishing
Ann Arbor, MI
www.cherrylakepublishing.com

Math Adviser: Tonya Walker, MA, Boston University

Nutrition Adviser: Steven Abrams, MD, Professor of Pediatrics, Baylor College of
Medicine, Houston, Texas

Photo Credits: Cover and page 1, © Randy Faris/CORBIS; page 6, © Tom and Dee Ann
McCarthy/CORBIS; page 10, Photo Courtesy of U. S. Department of Agriculture; page
17, © Ed Bock/CORBIS; page 25, © Rodney Hyett; Elizabeth Whiting & Associates/
CORBIS; page 27, Rodney Hyett; Elizabeth Whiting & Associates/CORBIS; page 27,
Ariel Skelley/CORBIS; page 28, Tom and Dee Ann McCarthy/CORBIS

Copyright ©2008 by Cherry Lake Publishing
All rights reserved. No part of this book may be reproduced or utilized in any
form or by any means without written permission from the publisher.

Library of Congress Cataloging-in-Publication Data
Minden, Cecilia.
  Breakfast by the numbers / by Cecilia Minden.
    p. cm.
  ISBN-13: 978-1-60279-011-7
  ISBN-10: 1-60279-011-6
  1. Breakfasts—Juvenile literature. I. Title.
  TX733.M56 2007
  642—dc22                                    2007003887

*Cherry Lake Publishing would like to acknowledge the work of*
*The Partnership for 21st Century Skills.*
*Please visit* www.21stcenturyskills.org *for more information.*

# TABLE of CONTENTS

## CHAPTER ONE

# WAKE-UP CALL

*Morning is a time to recharge your body's
batteries after a good night's sleep.*

You can't wait to hear your favorite song. You turn on your MP3 player,

but there is no sound. You probably need to recharge the battery. A battery

provides the power to listen to your music. Recharge the battery, and you

will soon be happily listening to your favorite tunes.

What does your body have in common with your MP3 player? Your body also won't work properly until it is "recharged." Not eating is called fasting. We are fasting while we are sleeping. Breakfast means to break the fast. Food is the fuel that recharges your body. The **calories** in the food you eat give your body energy. It is a signal to your body that you are up, moving, and ready to work and play.

But keep in mind that an MP3 player only needs a certain number of batteries for it to work. Taping extra batteries to the outside won't make it work any better. It just adds weight to the player. The same is true with your body. You only need a certain amount

Do you ever wonder why parents and teachers are always nagging you about eating breakfast? They have a few good reasons. Studies show that kids who eat breakfast get better grades in school and are more likely to exhibit good behavior.

How can you make sure you have time for breakfast? Get organized before you go to bed! Put out the clothes you will wear in the morning. Pack your backpack and leave it by the door. Can you think of some other things you can do to make time for a good breakfast?

of food each day based on your weight and level of activity. When you take

in more calories than your body needs, you gain weight. Your body also

works best when you take in calories throughout the day and don't load up

on calories all in one meal. The best place to start is at breakfast.

*Morning is a busy time, but it is important to try to eat a good breakfast.*

## CHAPTER TWO

# BREAKFAST OPTIONS

*Many people think of foods such as bacon, eggs, and toast when they think of breakfast.*

There are many foods that make up a healthy breakfast. And there

are many that don't. How do you choose the best foods for you? It isn't

difficult. It just takes a little time and effort.

Think of breakfast as the fuel your body needs for the day. Which gives

you more energy: a frozen pastry or a bowl of hot cereal? Pastry is like a

firecracker. It looks pretty, gives a big burst of energy, and then quickly

*A bowl of oatmeal with fruit can provide energy that will last all morning.*

fades away. Hot cereal is more like a strong battery. It fills you up and gives you power to last all morning.

Sitting down to eat not only helps your **digestion**, but it makes for a nice way to start the day. It gives you time to talk to your family and plan schedules. Taking time for breakfast gives the food a chance to start refueling your body before you even walk out the door. Here are some suggestions for a good breakfast at home:

- Whole grain cereal topped with fresh fruit and low-fat milk

- Whole grain toaster waffles with low-fat yogurt and fresh fruit

- Hot oatmeal with walnuts and blueberries

- Whole grain toast, eggs, and half a grapefruit

- Whole grain **tortilla** with scrambled eggs, cheese, and salsa

*Each color in the food pyramid represents a different food group.*
*Visit MyPyramid.gov to learn more about each group.*

Some mornings, there just isn't enough time to enjoy a leisurely

breakfast with your family. As hectic as the morning might be, you still

need to eat. You need a **nutritious** meal you can eat on the run. Here are

*21st CENTURY SKILLS LIBRARY*

some suggestions for a breakfast on the run:

- Peanut butter on whole wheat bread

- Smoothie made with low-fat milk and fruit

- Bag of trail mix (nuts, seeds, and dried fruit)

Keep in mind that these are just suggestions.

Is pizza one of your favorite foods? Look through some cookbooks and find a recipe for a breakfast pizza. Or make up your own breakfast pizza recipe. With a little planning, you can make just about any food part of a healthy breakfast.

## 21st Century Content

Visit MyPyramid.gov to learn more about how to choose healthy meals. The Food Pyramid there places foods in categories: grains, vegetables, fruit, milk, meat and beans, and oils.

Grains are foods made from wheat, rice, oats, barley, and other whole grains. Vegetables can be fresh, frozen, canned, or dried. Whole fruits or 100 percent fruit juice are a part of the fruit group. Milk and products made from milk, such as yogurt and cheese, are in the milk group. Foods in the meat and bean group include meat (beef and pork, for example), poultry, fish, nuts, eggs, and beans, such as black, kidney, and navy beans. The oils category includes liquid oils such as olive and canola oil, solid fats such as butter, and other foods high in fat content such as mayonnaise and salad dressings.

The Web site also includes information on serving sizes and how many servings you need from each food group every day.

There are many breakfast choices for you to make. The one choice you shouldn't make is skipping breakfast. Skipping breakfast will leave you feeling sleepy, tired, and grouchy. School and play deserve your full attention. It is hard to concentrate when your stomach is rumbling!

*You may find yourself falling asleep at school if you skip breakfast.*

*A look at the foods in your refrigerator or pantry
may give you some breakfast ideas.*

## REAL WORLD MATH CHALLENGE

Charlie looks in his kitchen to decide what to have for breakfast. He finds the following foods:

**Cereal:** Fruit Squares, Wheat Puffs, Oatmeal Swirls

**Drinks:** orange juice, milk, grape juice

**Fruit:** orange, peach, apple

**If he chooses one kind of cereal, one drink, and one fruit, how many different combinations could he create for his breakfast?**

*(Turn to page 29 for the answer)*

## CHAPTER THREE

# Do the Math: Breakfast at Home

*Drinking a glass of milk at breakfast can help you get the calcium your body needs.*

Are you ready for a delicious breakfast? Start by doing your best to select foods from a variety of food groups. Next, calculate the number of calories in each **portion**.

As you make your selections, keep in mind that an average 9- to 13-year-old needs 5 to 6 ounces (142 to 170 g) of grain, 2 to 2.5 cups of vegetables, 1.5 cups of fruit, 3 cups (750 ml) of milk, 5 ounces (142 g) of meat, and 5 teaspoons (25 ml) of fat each day. These should be spread throughout the day, typically in three meals and one or two snacks.

How big is a portion? Visualizing common objects may help you remember just how much you should eat. For example, 1 cup of potatoes, pasta, or rice is about the size of a tennis ball. A 3-ounce (85-gram) serving of meat is about the size of a deck of cards. A medium piece of fruit or 1 cup of leafy green vegetables is about the size of a baseball. A 1.5-ounce (42.5-g) serving of cheese is about the size of four stacked dice. And 1 teaspoon (5 milliliters) of oil is about the size of the tip of your thumb.

## REAL WORLD MATH CHALLENGE

James ate a breakfast of one scrambled egg, two pieces of toast, and 2 teaspoons (10 ml) of butter. He also had 1 cup (237 ml) of milk and one-half of a grapefruit. **Which food groups were represented in his breakfast? How many food groups were there in all?**

*(Turn to page 29 for the answers)*

The energy available in food is measured in calories. How many calories should you consume? An average 10- to 12-year-old needs about 2,000 calories a day. The exact amount you need depends on how active you are during the day. A very active person burns more calories. A less-active person uses less. If you eat more calories than your body uses in a day, the extra energy will be stored as fat in your body. In other words, you will gain weight.

## REAL WORLD MATH CHALLENGE

Lizzie's breakfast consists of 1 cup of Toasty Circles (100 calories) and ½ cup (118 ml) of low-fat milk (40 calories). She also had 1 cup (237 ml) of orange juice (120 calories).

**How many calories did Lizzie have for breakfast?**

**Lizzie normally takes in 2,000 calories a day. What percentage of her daily calories did she eat for breakfast?**

*(Turn to page 29 for the answers)*

*You will burn more calories each day if you are very active.*

## 21st Century Content

If you take in 3,500 more calories than you burn off, you will gain 1 pound (0.45 kilogram). A 12-ounce (355-ml) can of soda contains about 140 calories. One soda a day equals 4,200 extra calories a month. You could gain about 14 pounds (6.3 kg) in a year if you aren't active enough to burn off those calories!

## CHAPTER FOUR

# Do the Math: Fast-Food Breakfast

*It is okay to eat a breakfast sandwich from your favorite restaurant once in a while.*

Sometimes you may end up having breakfast away from home. Maybe you are traveling with your family. Maybe you have an away game and need to eat on the way. Whatever the reason, you are in a fast-food restaurant. You need to make a choice about breakfast. Knowing about

calories and portion sizes will help you choose something you like and

keep it healthy.

## REAL WORLD MATH CHALLENGE

When Lizzie goes to the Speedy Diner for breakfast, she typically eats twice as many calories as she would at home. **If she consumes 800 calories at the Speedy Diner, how many would she have at home?**

**Of her 2,000 daily calories, what percent does she eat when she has breakfast at the Speedy Diner?**

**What percent of her calories would she eat if she stayed home?**

(Turn to page 29 for the answers)

Did you know that a typical fast-food breakfast sandwich (biscuit, egg,

cheese, and sausage) has between 500 and 750 calories? A restaurant breakfast

of pancakes, syrup, butter, and sausage can add up to more than 1,000 calories.

Does that mean you should never eat breakfast at your favorite restaurants?

If you are making healthy food choices most of the time, an occasional high-calorie meal won't be a nutrition disaster. But you may want to think about what you eat the rest of the day—or get in a little more physical activity to burn off some of those extra calories!

# REAL WORLD MATH CHALLENGE

Let's go to the Bakery Breakfast Bar. Everything smells so good! You choose a big cinnamon bagel (360 calories), honey-walnut cream cheese (140 calories), and a large hot chocolate (650 calories).

**How many calories does that breakfast add up to?**

**Compare that to the 2,000 calories your body needs each day. What percent of your total did you use?**

**Which foods groups did you choose foods from?**

**Which food groups were left out?**

(Turn to page 29 for the answers)

*Restaurants offer many options for healthy and not-so-healthy breakfasts.*

Restaurants are fun places to spend time with your family and

friends. It is a nice break when no one has to cook or clean up. Let's take

a look at some other choices at the Bakery Breakfast Bar. If you choose

a smaller bagel (150 calories), a tablespoon of low-fat cream cheese

(32 calories), a glass of low-fat milk (120 calories), and a small apple

(45 calories), your meal will add up to 347 calories. That is a delicious

breakfast with about the same number of calories as just one big

cinnamon bagel.

Does that mean you should never eat a big cinnamon bagel with that

yummy honey-walnut cream cheese? Of course not! Just remember that

*You can enjoy a big cinnamon bagel once in a*
*while. Just make sure it isn't every day!*

*People who make food look good in photographs are called food stylists.*

Restaurant menus are full of beautiful pictures of tempting food. You want to choose them all! That's thanks to the work of a professional food stylist. A food stylist prepares food for photographs. However, some foods fade or melt under hot camera lights. To keep the food looking tasty, food stylists use a variety of special effects. Mashed potatoes are often substituted for ice cream, cereal floats in white glue instead of milk, and cake stays fresh looking when hair spray is applied. So next time you look at a restaurant menu, take a closer look at those pictures. Then ask yourself what you are REALLY looking at!

you always have choices, and it is up to you to keep

your food choices balanced.

## CHAPTER FIVE

# OFF TO A GREAT START!

*An apple can be part of a healthy breakfast on the run.*

Morning, especially on a school day, is a very busy time in everyone's household. You have to get dressed, load up your backpack, fix your lunch, find your shoes, and maybe even get in some last-minute studying. Breakfast can easily turn into something you eat in the car on the way to school—or something you skip altogether. But with

a little planning, your entire family can make some changes that will help

everyone get the day off to a good start.

Use the ideas in this book to help you get started. Check out some

cookbooks from your family's bookshelf or the library. Become a label

reader. Look for food that is low in fat and sugar and made from whole

grains. Talk to your mom and dad about helping you stock the pantry

with nutritious breakfast foods. Chances are, you already have many good

choices in your home.

Before you go to bed, get organized for the next morning's breakfast.

Put out cups, bowls, and **utensils**. Have all of the foods you need ready in

the refrigerator or on the counter, if they won't spoil. That way you will

have more time to enjoy your breakfast in the morning.

*Setting out bowls and utensils the night before can
help you make time for a healthy breakfast.*

What about those mornings when you have to leave extra early

because you have a club meeting, band or chorus rehearsal, or sports team

practice? You can prepare a healthy breakfast, put it in a bag, and leave it

in the refrigerator. In the morning, all you'll have to do is grab the bag and

go. Breakfast on the run is definitely preferable to no breakfast at all!

By planning ahead, you won't spend your mornings searching for something to eat. Include a variety of foods in your plans. Eating the same thing day after day will get boring. And remember, the best-laid plans sometimes don't work out. Keep some prepared foods in the pantry and refrigerator to use as backup on mornings when something unexpected throws everything off.

*Early morning activities such as band practice can
make it hard to fit in a good breakfast.*

Breakfast bars made from whole grains and dried fruit, single-serving packages of cereal, and easily portable whole fruits can be good choices.

Aim for a breakfast rich in nutrients from all of the food groups on most mornings. That is the best way to break your fast. You will feel energized and ready to face whatever challenges the day might bring.

*A good breakfast helps prepare you for the day ahead!*

# REAL WORLD MATH CHALLENGE ANSWERS

## Chapter Two

### Page 13

Charlie can make 27 different combinations of foods for his breakfast.

$3 \times 3 \times 3 = 27$

## Chapter Three

### Page 15

James had foods from 5 food groups:

Meat and beans (eggs)

Grain (toast)

Oils (butter)

Milk

Fruit (grapefruit)

### Page 16

Lizzie had 260 calories at breakfast.

$100 + 40 + 120 = 260$

If Lizzie normally takes in 2,000 calories each day, this breakfast represents 13 percent of her daily calories.

$260 \div 2,000 = 0.13 = 13\%$

## Chapter Four

### Page 19

Lizzie usually consumes 400 calories for breakfast when she eats at home.

$800 \div 2 = 400$

The 800 calories she consumes at the Speedy Diner represent 40 percent of her daily calories.

$800 \div 2,000 = 0.40 = 40\%$

If Lizzie stayed home and ate 400 calories for breakfast, she would consume 20 percent of her daily calories.

$400 \div 2,000 = 0.20 = 20\%$

### Page 20

The Bakery Breakfast Bar meal add ups to 1,150 calories.

$360 + 140 + 650 = 1,150$

If you normally consume 2,000 calories a day, this meal represents 58 percent of your calories for the day.

$1,150 \div 2,000 = 0.575 = 58\%$

This meal has foods from the grain, meat and bean, and milk groups.

It doesn't contain foods from the fruit, vegetable, and oil groups.

# GLOSSARY

**calories (KAL-uh-reez)** the measurement of the amount of energy available to your body in the food you eat

**digestion (dih-JESS-chuhn)** the process of breaking down food in your stomach and other organs so that it can be used by your body

**nutritious (new-TRISH-uss)** adding value to one's diet by contributing to health or growth

**portion (POR-shuhn)** a part or share of something; enough of one kind of food to serve someone at a meal

**poultry (POHL-tree)** birds that are raised for their meat and eggs; chickens, turkeys, ducks, and geese are poultry

**tortilla (tor-TEE-uh)** round, flat bread that is made from cornmeal or flour

**utensils (yoo-TEN-suhlz)** tools used for eating or preparing food

# For More Information

## Books

Lagasse, Emeril, and Charles Yuen (illustrator). *There's a Chef in My Soup! Recipes for the Kid in Everyone.* New York: HarperCollins, 2002.

Nissenberg, Sandra K., and Heather Nissenberg. *I Made It Myself! Mud Cups, Pizza Puffs, and Over 100 Other Fun and Healthy Recipes for Kids to Make.* New York: Wiley, 1998.

## Web Sites

### NutritionExplorations.org—Kids Activities
*www.nutritionexplorations.org/kids/activities-main.asp*
Includes shopping lists, food trackers, and activities that teach facts about nutrition

### United States Department of Agriculture—MyPyramid.gov
*www.mypyramid.gov/*
Information on the various food groups and tips for healthy eating

# INDEX

## ABOUT THE AUTHOR

**Cecilia Minden**, PhD, is a literacy consultant and the author of many books for children. She is the former director of the Language and Literacy Program at Harvard Graduate School of Education in Cambridge, Massachusetts. She would like to thank fifth-grade math teacher Beth Rottinghaus for her help with the Real World Math Challenge problems. Cecilia lives with her family in North Carolina.

EAST ORANGE PUBLIC LIBRARY

3 2665 0037 1322 1

j642 MIN
Minden, Cecilia DISCARD
Breakfast by the numbers

7/08